SEEING
Hummingbird
Move

KASEY C. JONES

AuthorHouse™
1663 Liberty Drive
Bloomington, IN 47403
www.authorhouse.com
Phone: 1 (800) 839-8640

This book is printed on acid-free paper.

ISBN: 978-1-7283-6324-0 (sc)
ISBN: 978-1-7283-6323-3 (e)

Library of Congress Control Number: 2020909789

Print information available on the last page.

Published by AuthorHouse 05/28/2020

authorHOUSE®

....17

....19

....20

ds and Goddesses 22

thering You? 23

ecipice 24

er Time 25

or of Puissance 26

wo Is Communal 27

Tone 28

My Solemn Dissolve 29

Fragile Limbs 30

Some Mix Of 31

Instead of the Usual 33

On the Heels of Love 34

Fast Burger 35

My Thoughts 37

High Element 38

Contents

Soothing Hummingbird ....

The Taste..

My Many ....

The Purest Me ....

Your Lunch ....

Not a Poem ....

Whistle Sounds...

Flute.. 11

Never Been Around the World... 12

Dance 13

I've Seen People Cut Cake Before... 14

I Forgive Everyone.. 15

Necessary Steps.. 16

Dismantled ....

Be Quiet ....

To the River ...

Children, G

What's Bo

Off a Pr

Anoth

Col

T

Dad...39

Now..40

Noteworthy..41

My Heart..42

Birds Are Here...43

I Think Like a Twig..45

Little Piece Of Grass..46

I Can Taste the Fog...47

Sneezing Myself Into The Ocean..48

Roll Like A Butterfly...49

No Frozen Sweaters...50

Sparkling..51

Bedridden Thoughts..52

Music Highlights..53

Goodbye Piñata..54

Unpin the Clouds...55

Soothing Hummingbird

My name is Fady, all I have is water to drink,

When water is what I decided to reach for

In the cupboard.

My Stones are precious jewels, crystals

My wind frames of fish I once ate, before famine came.

The Famine released me from my marriage, killing them

With a mountain shaped like a spear, and now I'm a grand

Star in the sea.

My name is Fady, all I have is water to drink.

Yes. Nothing but water, even in my dreams my poetry is

New color.

The Taste

Everything tastes much greener than ever to Rodger,
An assortment that shrill voice loves;
That shrill voice loves it.
Everything oozes an awesome daily freshness
That cannot be explained, not even with a shrill voice.

Everything is the taste of ice, salt heat and nothingness,
An assortment if I peer over the mountain after I've
Climbed up the counter looking through the Sun but
Hard away from the Curtains.

Everything I can swallow even things that cannot be explained,
It is simply the taste I want, the taste I enjoy,
The taste I merge into.

*M*y Many

Melissa says, the purple of her rainbow
Lands in no pot of coins.

The red of her rainbow
Is not cloth for his loins.

Melissa says, the boundaries of light blue
Rests just above her name.

The simple and true
Is painting her the same.

The mass penalties
Are points on a black-board.

The youthful children and kitties,
Baskets for the good cord.

Wake up this nation
Unto youthful voices,

Sling a royal vacation
To her many choices.

The Purest Me

Winter's little crying black, behind a peak
And now I think that sorrow to actually
Be songs sang to me and all who care to see.

Winter's little crying black is just
Summer's big singing white dove and is
Autumn's mediocre dancing girl in a red dress:
Spring's mediocre breathing boy cutting wood
With green mold on it.

Winter's little crying black, behind a peak,
Who are you and what do you have for me.

Your Lunch

I glance at this bottled water and now,

I jot down your order, the stars, the

Sky as a zodiac sign, you just might

Remind me a little of Mars.

I can compensate a stream for a lonesome

Bored ocean, the fish, this cloudy blue

Giving things a flow. This door closing as I realize you only would like another

Water and a spinach salad sprinkled with

Pepper, cheese, a bowl, a fork

For Heaven's sake. You wait alone patiently

Fearing the foods shrinkage and a ease

Heat warming your lunch.

Not a Poem

At a point in time
I feel mostly drawings both male and
Female. In the past I would tear
Beaming and it's all at a tone of
Thrill. I get intensely selfish
With a bunch of scribbles.

Whistle Sounds

Two melodies submerged in a whistle wood,
And my apologies to circumvent that sound it should
Be one song over the other and have my ears
Listen. Choosing the Higher pitch that vibrates
Heightens itself in loops, as I hear moving music.

Though as for the quieter melody goes
Soft and brief I must not hear too much glows
Just brighter is the first musical sound which
Clearly warms my earlobes and makes a sandwich
With them,

And these two melodic tunes dance free because
The days are dry without them, the days will pause
So that I might sift through the wonderful noise.
Yes, I study this music and it forms toys
In my mind but really in my need to breathe.

lute

What could it be, that feels so good,
That steals my attention. I believe
It lives somewhere near passion but
Hand in hand with excitement. I'm
So glad that you called lingering like
Silver and blue in something that
I might drink. Don't be bashful, I'm
Inviting you to stay so that I can
Continue analyzing these results, these
Feelings that are changing my life.
If it were an instruments sound, it would
Be a flute and a violin and perhaps a
Xylophone. If it were a taste, it would
Be air and jam on a freshly baked
Slice of bread. I can dance with you
On my boat of empty thoughts and rest
Assured you're a gift from the cosmos.

Never Been Around the World

I've never been to the Great Wall

Or the pyramids.

I've never been to the statue of liberty

Or Niagara Falls.

I've never been to Grand Rapids

Or Syria.

You don't need ask me about Africa

Or Atlanta because someone from

Olympia asked you to.

Don't sing that song,

Don't bother me at all,

Never been around the world.

Dance

The day I heard you dance like a tiger bird, there,
Dipping and tip-toeing freshly where
The linen covers compelling us to listen covertly.
The movements of you I ate for motion up late
As you leave nothing too easily broken.
The sheets of paper were pregnant with infants
That roll off the tongue.
This plastic bottle of milk collected the feel
Meant for the blood and carried vowels
For each day.
The day I heard you dance like a tiger bird the
White sheets were being kicked and shifted
To spell it's another girl.

I've Seen People Cut Cake Before

This minuscule declaration that I know is also true for you.

I've seen people cut cake before, honey and so have you.

The moist yellow crumbles or whatever color you please,

I know that soft goodness just as still as can be or hypnotizing me.

Don't you remember the last time by the pool with the balloons

And the children brightly. Yes honey, I do that was so special in

My memories, I was a child but I can still see that as if it happened

This morning.

I Forgive Everyone

Playing in the sand, playing in the dirt,
Playing in the rain, playing in the water,
I forgive everyone, and let everyone forgive
Me. I forgive everyone and anyone who
Has ever failed me.

Tasting on the floor, tasting on the home-front,
Tasting on the base, tasting on the confidence
That my candy forgives me and my indulgence
Into lightly colored sweets is like my constant with
Tea.

Necessary Steps

At the age of twenty six, I am in the Army
And I am a bit over the average age. Am I too
Old to eat chow with these guys who allow me
To talk with them all day and grow the inch with
Them? Should I regret waiting so long to join, was
I wrong when I completed the necessary steps and
Filling in the Army Reps before those unmentioned
Deadlines? Why am I putting my mind and body
Through tough times just because I'm getting good
Dimes? My fellow soldiers are simply doing the same
Thing, no matter what they tell you. We are enclosed
In this large tight room with some boys writing letters,
Others running, playing around and some talking or telling
Jokes to compare whose is better between bunkmates.
I remember we could only drink water, I'd gladly eat a
Wafer because sweets was shunned, unless it was in our juice.
We carried water containers around with us, we said good-bye
To being a gamer and hello to this soldier training camp.

This was the art of being part of Basic Training in the Army, and
That was just the start of it, the bit that I am only willing to
Mention.

Dismantled

I fastened sticks of dynamite
Of my favorite color purple to
My tuxedo as I chose to
Climax while wearing these fluffy
Earmuffs. I may look unstoppable
At first glance but then you'll
Realize that a bomb squad (or
Whatever they're called) will swoop
Down in and quickly dismantle my life
Or what's left of it.

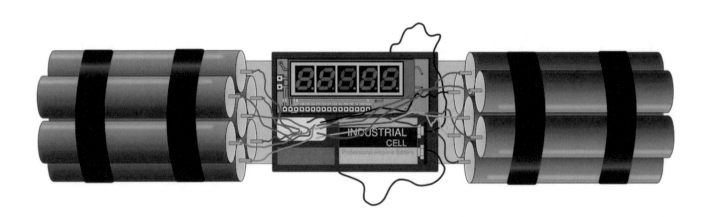

Be Quiet

The citrus in my soft citrine-like lemons
Are complete like the lines on that
Chalkboard spelling "be quiet", my music
Teacher humorously wrote, almost as a
Way to entertain us eager and open-minded
Kids (like astute sponges soaking up soda).
No one has ever crestfallen in her class,
We were strangely energized but motionless
At the same time like, there was always some
Lava in her coffee mug producing rainbow
Colored honeycombs as her music class
Assignments that we could look at with
Telescopes.

To the River

There is no stone in my soup.
I do not walk down to the river,
Instead I jog or scurry.
There is no burnt clay to use for
My sculpting.
I do not forget to laugh at the
Playground after lunch.

One must ask the question, must I
Shine so brightly as a diamond would
Or should I reduce myself to a mere
Rock and should I care to even ask this
Question to myself?

There is no stone in my soup but
I see many stones in the river and
Lying sporadically at the playground.
There is no need for a stone to be in
My lunch but I do remember reading
About such a stone in elementary
School and I believe the book was called
"Stone Soup with Rice".

Children, Gods and Goddesses

And if I should have children,
Know that you are guaranteed
Highs and lows, loves and
Disappointments but also you will
Learn to dance and you will dance
To the fact that you are like Kings
And Queens, Gods and Goddesses
And you are Unstoppable and
Destined for an adventure that
Only the cosmos already understand,
You are certain to appreciate things
That will stick to your bones like the
Old saying about Oatmeal. If you
Should need help, I will hope that I
Could solve it. If you should ask me
For assistance, I will try to be there in
A jiffy. If I am mown and off the grid,
I will be confident that there will be
No pieces of you to pick up, at least
Until you've had enough of the sun.

What's Bothering You?

When my mother let me see her cry,
You would expect the distance between
Us to die, and it did to a certain extent.
I could not fathom what it was that was
Opposed to dwindling away (from her
And us). She let me see her cry but I was
Still and silent. I never felt a feeling of
Wanting to say something as much as I
Did at that time, (for what I can
Remember) and I never had the syllables
Prepped for caressing her emotion. I felt
As useless as a simple dandelion and as
Powerless as a fried computer. When my
Mother let me see her cry, I knew that
Deep down it had to be a sign of trust or
Either it was that she could no longer hold
The pain, but I chose to feel connected
With her; so that I would never forget that
Day.

Off a Precipice

Here you come, leaving nostalgia behind; from
A wanderjahr with your jar of a thousand pennies
As if they're your offered tidings, or as if you
Thought I to be clergy and your coins were your
Tithings. I believe you walked off a precipice when
You assumed I was going to count all that. I get
Paid minimum wage for what it's worth; I don't
Recall my boss approving me to process you in this
Situation. Please do not rest that glass at the check
Out unless it's hollowed out. My chest unnoticeably
Just caved in a bit but there is a glimmer of hope that
I will be rummaging home to eat my spinach salad
And its mishpocha.

Another Time

It's just a coincidence how we clashed
With our arches of wind demystifying
Inertia. I'm picturing myself as an aged
Bird nuzzled for meager crumbs. You
Are with me as a cloud, a fellow
Daily-breader that I've never met before
But seen many similar forms. You
Welcome our plight and apologize for the
Collision. I accept as I awake from the
Dream to be fading back into the real me.
I only recall brushes of our journey that I
Transport to paint and paper in little
Clumps. We ended our day rainy with tears
But I know I'll see you again in another
Time.

Color of Puissance

Stand tall flags of puissance,
America once implored your stars,
Stripes, blood, violence, tea, drinks,
Rights, voices, television, telephone,
Radio, politicians, teachers, scholars,
Doctors and onward.
Stand tall inexcusable rib-cage of the
World or at least that's what you once
Tried to be. It's been many days you've
Set aside your stethoscope and deduced
That you knew better and laughed
Because your rhapsodies looked yellower.

Two Is Communal

He treated you with an
Unapologetic hate. A
Hate that can grow and taint.

She was happy to ruin
Your incredible day. A
Day of January, the middle.

But this new man for you is
Melodious equanimity,
This new future woman wants
You with congruence tantalizing.
The time has come for the stitches
To crumble, let's acknowledge, that
Five great people await you nearby
For every one nasty rock of a person/
Relationship that is destined for zero.

You will be communal.

one

I wore a bespectacled tone,
My face transcends sound on
This drive in a car expelling
The sunlight. I am sitting here
In the backseat picturing a
Folktale in my Notepad; that's
Incomplete. How can you
Encompass each detail in a short
Drawing. I sense a diminution in
My will to tell their story but
Instead recreate it for myself.

My Solemn Dissolve

My solemn dissolve of obdurate
Baggage has seldom brought sore
Feelings of bore and grief. There
Was not much need to reconcile a
Particular status regarding a person
Because I always felt less than
Picturesque in circumference. My
Early years left a disheartening air
On my lips and eyes so I chose to
Wear a stealth mask like backwards
Hair, irresolute that it was always in
Place and up for the task. I was
Remediable and confused as to why
I wanted to hide my authentic
Characteristics.

Fragile Limbs

My fragile limbs are hovering above,
Hovering above me, hovering above.
My fragile knees are beneath me,
Somewhere beneath me, beneath me.
The energy that traces north
Meditates with falling water and me
In mind. The disarmingly conversational
Energy traces us accessible and
Completive with frailty.

Some Mix Of

Just some mix of
Pecan pie of
Brown Khakis of
Car vacuumed of
Pair of boots of
Gold trimmed watch of
Fresh tint. Shades of
Long trench-coat, the

Same these things here.

Instead of the Usual

My flames have just been exponential,
Extramural is just the phoenix
I am, while just wearing a dress shirt
And so as the double agent just
Destitute in a dream just appeased
By what I was just given, wrapped up
In this needy dialect that just
Contaminates just community.
I remember just my own power,
I disprove just al dente noodles,
It's just accusatory, my smell
Offends you, adhesive to just shame
On my name just abysmal you think
Of me. I just phoenix rises soon.

On the Heels of Love

I find myself illegible to
The feeling of my eyes, I entail
A hieroglyphic hunk of lovely
Love.

I'm not reaching inwards for my back-
Scratcher.

I can omit the thought of intervening
As a lighthouse, (as if I'm better).

No one can beat my kiwi cool aiding
Drink and julep.

At any time I could hydroplane
Inept; inlet an incantation.
I refuse to humping be Kaput.

Fast Burger

Big bulge and meat grease,
Marinating, teasing me,
Begging boy to bite.

*M*y Thoughts

Your face is prepared, for my thoughts
And even the cracks in them that
Cause laughter, silence and some pain.

This atmosphere you sink into
My life speaks of cooked birds and words
Causing laughs; rest for champions.

Cheek to cheek, around our softness,
Sometimes ignoring the cracks; words
That laugh at us and our deep love.

High Element

I may walk on top, to slice
Into my package of sun.
The shine wildly dispersed must
Carve a smile easily on
My bare face.

I will feel security
Like no exposed spider could
Imagine.

I can learn to make a grand
Incision like winter does
To Autumn with milky white
Element.

I will feel security
Like no exposed spider could
Imagine.

Dad

I informed my Dad
On his special day, that mom
Had forgotten him.

My Dad replied soft
On his special day, that mom
Was a greedy monster.

Dad did not say this,
But, I knew by default and
By wordings before.

ow

Crumbs of sand gnawing

At the early blue ocean

My heart ablaze now.

Noteworthy

I hear the tone of
Your aura, when you walk by,
It is noteworthy.

Your tone is higher
Than mine, is it due to I'm
Male and you are not?

I wonder does tone
Affect the amount of joy,
This is noteworthy.

My Heart

My Heart roars like a car,

Beep, beep, I'm coming to get you.

My heart soars like a mountain.

My mountain flies down the street.

My car points upward into the clouds.

My horn roars like a mountain

My frost melts like the tires at my feet.

I love being me.

Birds Are Here

Birds are here, birds are there,
Birds are everywhere, birds are here,
Birds are there, birds are everywhere
We want to be. Birds are here,
Birds are there, birds are everywhere,
Come and see. I am a bird and
So are you. We are birds in the air,
We are birds in the air,
Listen to my singing voice, I am a bird.
Listen to my singing voice, I am a bird,
Can't you see. I am a bird, I am a bird,
I am a bird, I am a bird.

I Think Like a Twig

I think like a twig, excuse me

Are you talking to me.

I think like a twig, is it me, is it me.

I think like a twig, excuse me,

Are you talking to me, I think like a twig,

Is it just us here, you and me. I think like a twig,

Excuse me, excuse me, I think like a twig.

Are you a friend of the fly resting on me.

I think like a twig, excuse me, excuse me.

I think like a twig, you are a lovely thing to see.

Little Piece Of Grass

Little piece of grass, my, how we have grown.

We have seen the wonders of the world.

We have traveled to places unknown.

We have gotten married, we have had kids,

We have buried our parents,

We have raised our neighbor's kids.

My little piece of grass, how we have grown.

I Can Taste the Fog

I can taste the fog.
The fog tastes of secrets
And berries on an obvious day.

Wouldn't you like a taste?
Wouldn't you like to relax with
A cold drink of lemonade, and
Feel the warmth of the fog?
Couldn't you sit next to a mushroom,
Next to a rock, on top of grass, on top
Of dirt? Wouldn't you rest under layers
Of white cloudy mist and green leaves?
Yes, I tell you, I can taste the fog. What a
Splendid day.

Sneezing Myself Into The Ocean

It's okay, mom didn't mean it, she was just drunk.

It's okay, that politician was taken out of context,
He loves all people.

It's okay, that scandal with the pictures of people
Being tortured, they must have done something to
Deserve it.

It's okay, we don't have to hold people accountable
For their actions.

Really, is it really okay, sneezing myself into the ocean.

Roll Like A Butterfly

I like to be both mysterious and obvious;

I like to roll with the punches and punch back
Useless critiques.

I am my own archetype sheet but my grace
May be familiar like a butterfly with color and
Knees.

Don't pet me, I am not a dog. Just watch and be
Amazed as I clear your mushy fog.

No Frozen Sweaters

It seems some people wear cobwebs
To fight freezing words while I
Adorn myself in grand sweaters to
Ward off their nighty nights. I'm far
From the age of nineteen and there's
No need to shiver on their account.
I'll take their jokes and sly mumbles
Into my suitcase; fold them up and
Barf it all into my memory bag as I
Think of them sliding 'round in their
Coffin.

I'm taking a walk to seek Mr. Jolly or
Mr. Rancher. So that I can replace those
Useless thoughts out for Mr. Star and ask
If Mr. Burst can come along.

Sparkling

I've charred my love of art scrunched
In my ponytails. I gargle fresh minty
Excess, but never a redundant sex;
Possibly the middle, and you'll never find
My teeth as your sparkling mantelpiece.

You've barred my eyesight in preference
Of someone whom is a tardy mess.
You hate me being too blunt but loves
Their riddles, you're not too keen on
Barking cats.

I've harvested your tomatoes, studied
Them as a one member class. You've
Branched out of me with flesh and mass.
If I were both a sandwich and a
Bowling ball, I'd be full of glitter,
Diamonds, engraved streamers and
Purple paper lettuce.

Run to the front of the line, share
A ring from my hair and have a
Gay rolling; posing time.

Bedridden Thoughts

I possibly had a moldy upbringing,
A journey of a smelly vehicle.
I courted concessions that amounted
To zero.
I became an evocative flame;
A raging; hard ocean.
I knew something had to be done
To make me a better son, a powerful
Seed.
I fancied prestige a bit too much
And overly cared about reputations.

So is this what you'll do?

I certainly was careful and careless
As I drifted in a moldy vehicle.
I befriended my familial staff of
Lawyers, judges and the jury to help
Me sink and rise, before my realization to
Form my own opinions and learn to float.

So dear one, will you follow a similar
Path as me or will you fly beyond your
Hopes and dreams.

Music Highlights

Already having what I want,
I live my life as if I'm living under
The microscope of the Universe.
Living my life with a verse,
Reaching for the words often
Without music.
Spreading out my desires with music
Highlights to show my passion.
On occasion I am drenched in music,
Wet to any fires of doubt,
Luminous to an uplifting office
And I say to you "I am free from
Absurd restraints".

Goodbye Piñata

Shocking candy hearts, crashing down
Becoming a demolished part,
Opposed to frowns.
Yes! A Lexus, worn out bow,
Goodbye Piñata.
Now, I'm riding on top of a train
With a sprinkle of lightning on the
Wheels, POW!
My excitement rhymes with teal and is
Not fake.
Goodbye Piñata,
You were more than a friendly kite meant
To wine and dine for the day.
I know now that you were here
To heal and yes, you guessed it, so real.

Unpin the Clouds

As a child I suspected that
My mother did not unpin the
Clouds, but she somehow
Could very well make me feel as
Though she did. She could make
I feel as if those clouds, yes the ones
That mattered, were on the edge
Of something. I could feel that her very
Departure, was lava erupting from
An all-encompassing volcano, and that
Nothing could stop my
Dreadful pain and pouring tears.

I was young, silly, inexperienced,
At the helm of an odd youth
Balancing my frosted
Mannerisms and that was my
New world at the time.

Printed in the United States
By Bookmasters